A Sea Road to Rothesay

Ian McCrorie

Caledonian MacBrayne
Hebridean & Clyde Ferries

The well known but splendid image of the original Wemyss Bay pier with the fleet around 1875: from left to right *Largs, Lancelot, Lady Gertrude* and *Argyle*

J Adamson & Son, Rothesay.

Foreword

By
Dr Harold Mills CB
Chairman of Caledonian MacBrayne Ltd

Following the opening of Wemyss Bay pier and station in 1865, the steamer service between Wemyss Bay and Rothesay became one of the most important routes on the Firth of Clyde. Today it is the busiest crossing operated by Caledonian MacBrayne with about 750,000 passengers and 150,000 cars being carried between Wemyss Bay and Rothesay in 2004.

Over the years, Ian McCrorie, the Company's Historian, has written a series of books describing the development of the shipping services to the many islands served by the Company. It is appropriate that the Company should commission him to write a book recording the 140 years of the route to Rothesay from Wemyss Bay and fitting that it should be published at the same time as the new vessel, *Bute*, takes over service.

In this book, Ian McCrorie recalls the many Companies and ships which have served on the route, with successive generations of paddle steamers and turbine steamers giving way to the car ferries of today. The introduction of *Bute* is particularly significant. Her predecessor of the same name provided the first car ferry service to the Island of Bute with the vehicles being driven from the pier on to a lift at any state of the tide and subsequently parked in a spacious garage beneath the passenger accommodation. The service was modernised in the 1970s when the trio of vessels known affectionately as "the Streakers" entered service. They introduced a roll-on roll-off service for cars but, with their limited capacity and sideloading at Rothesay, they are now obsolescent. With the advent of *Bute*, a level of service appropriate to the 21st century will become available for foot passengers and cars.

Having served in the late 1950s on the previous *Bute* as an Assistant Purser to well known Rothesay Purser Peter Shaw and with a ship called *Bute* again operating between Wemyss Bay and Rothesay, I am particularly pleased to have the opportunity to write this foreword.

We are indebted to Ian McCrorie for producing a comprehensive account with its pictorial record of the many ships which have served on the route. I hope that all with memories of sailing between Wemyss Bay and Rothesay, past and present, will enjoy reading it.

June 2005

WEMYSS BAY.

An etching of the old pre-railway Wemyss Bay pier, showing Kelly House in the background.

Banks & Co., Edinburgh

The original two-funnelled paddle steamer *Bute* which sailed to and from Wemyss Bay in the first season, 1865

From a drawing in Mr Hubbard's collection

Rothesay in the 1860s

Early in the nineteenth century Rothesay was a fishing village with quite a substantial fifty year old harbour. In fact, since 1400, it had been a Royal Burgh and had boasted a fine castle since Norman times. The Brandanes, as the islanders of Bute are called, first saw the unusual spectacle of a steamship in 1814 or 1815, but at this time Largs and the Ayrshire townships were more fashionable as holiday destinations and it was several years before Rothesay came into its own as the premier resort on the Firth of Clyde.

As the Industrial Revolution progressed, more and more people migrated from the Highlands and from Ireland into the great city that Glasgow had become, but as the pace of change was too fast for sustainable growth, poverty and deprivation were the inevitable results. Every so often, during "Fast Days" and "Fair Holidays", the artisans were able to leave the grime of the city and make for the unspoiled firth on their doorstep. Rothesay, centred round a most scenic and sheltered bay, became the favourite destination and more and more flocked there during these few special days. Originally, the crowds sailed from the Broomielaw, in the heart of the city, but from 1841 the Glasgow, Paisley & Greenock Railway won through to the coast and an alternative mode of transport, by train and steamship, took off. Competition was intense and, inevitably, fares came down and traffic went up. It cost a mere 6d (2.5p) to sail 'doon the watter' from Glasgow to Greenock by one of the rival steamboats.

Not only was there intense competition between steamboat and railway but also between the steamboats themselves, the fifties and sixties seeing the most excessive rivalry. Racing, raw in its fervour, paid scant regard to the comfort of the passengers, but there is no doubt that the spectacle was most exhilarating. On one occasion, one of the fliers, the *Rothesay Castle*, made the passage from the Broomielaw to Rothesay, with the usual stops, in a mere 2 hours 28 minutes, a feat unrivalled before or since. Several of the fastest ships, however, were soon spirited away to America to run the Yankee blockade for the Confederates in the Civil War and by the middle of the decade a certain calmness had returned to the Firth. It was at this time that an alternative route to

An interior shot of the old Wemyss Bay station, built in 1865

An exterior shot of the old Wemyss Bay station building, taken from the north, or Rothesay, berth of the original railway pier

Rothesay was opened – via the Renfrewshire village of Wemyss Bay (pronounced 'Weems', or 'Wimms' by the locals).

The Coming of the Wemyss Bay Railway

In November 1862 construction started on a new single line railway which left what was now the main Caledonian Railway line to Greenock just west of Port Glasgow, climbed behind Greenock and then descended through the Kip Valley to a proposed new railhead at Wemyss Bay, a little to the south of the pier which already existed to service the Kelly Estate. The omens were good as the journey time between Glasgow and Rothesay would be slashed compared with travelling all the way by steamboat or connecting through the Greenock Railway. The Wemyss Bay Steamboat Co. Ltd. was formed to supply the steamer connections. The new company ordered two large saloon paddle steamers from the prestigious Caird's yard at Greenock and a smaller vessel for the all-year-round trade from Wingate's of Glasgow. One of the larger twins was actually sold to the Americans before she was launched but a new keel was soon laid down to replace her.

The larger *Kyles* and the smaller *Largs* were ready in good time for the opening of the line to the public on Monday 15 May 1865. The previous Saturday, with great pomp and circumstance, the directors and their friends had travelled over the line and connected into the *Kyles* for a cruise to Arran. The *Kyles* was now based at Tighnabruaich, appropriately in the Kyles of Bute, and sailed via Rothesay to connect with the train to Glasgow (Bridge Street Station) at 0810. She spent the day on that run, making three trips to and from Rothesay and two to the Kyles. The sad fact was that the ship did not come up to expectation as regards speed and so regularly ran late, which caused further delays. The trains frequently lost their slot on the Greenock line east of Port Glasgow and, more importantly, on the busy line between Paisley and Glasgow, which the Caledonian shared with the rival Glasgow & South Western Railway.

On 1 June 1865 a smaller second-hand steamboat was added to the Wemyss Bay fleet – Captain Duncan Stewart's economical *Victory* (1863). This tried and tested vessel should have brought improvement to the service but instead she heralded further expansion. The *Kyles* now lay at

Ardrishaig on Lochfyneside overnight and gave the main express connecting services morning and evening from and to Rothesay, the Kyles and Loch Fyne. The pier at Port Bannatyne just round the bay from Rothesay (opened in 1857) also received a call. The *Victory* looked after the service during the day while the larger vessel set off on a cruise. The arrival of the second large saloon steamer *Bute* in late June ushered in a further spreading of resources, with the *Kyles* now extending her daily journey from Loch Fyne to Glasgow, as if in competition with the trains. The upshot was economic disaster, with the sale of the *Kyles* and *Bute* at the end of the season inevitable.

Extravagance was replaced by prudence in 1866. The two remaining paddle steamers, *Largs* and *Victory*, were augmented by the *Argyle* (1866), from the same stable as the latter, and the three proceeded to give a much more realistic and less ambitious service to Rothesay, Largs and Millport. Despite the obvious improvement, poor management, and perhaps the fact that the engines on the Wemyss Bay line were underpowered in the early days, did not endear the company to the travelling public and the Wemyss Bay Steamboat Company was forced into liquidation early in 1869.

Gillies & Campbell

The Wemyss Bay directors had no alternative but to approach the various steamboat captains on the river with a view to their providing connecting services from the new railhead. These captains, however, thought that they could bring about the demise of their hated competitor and did not cooperate. The master of the *Largs*, Captain James Gillies, however, expressed an interest in sailing in connection with the Wemyss Bay trains and, along with his son-in-law Alexander Campbell, entered into an agreement with the directors in August 1869. Gillies already owned the *Venus* of 1852 and now acquired the *Largs, Victory* and *Argyle* from the liquidator. With these four worthy but unglamorous ships, Gillies and Campbell commenced a twenty-year association with the Wemyss Bay route. Their ships were austere, with black hulls and white funnels with black tops, and they ran a no-frills service for twelve months in the year – but their main feature was reliability, at least initially.

The service expanded steadily, with newer boats replacing the older units in the fleet. The *Victory* was sold in the spring of 1871 and replaced a year later with the company's first newbuild, the *Lady Gertrude*, named after the daughter of the Earl of Glasgow. Sadly she did not last long in the fleet: on Saturday 13 January 1877, in a severe gale, she was lost by stranding at Toward Pier, after her engine refused to respond to her master's instructions. Two years prior to this, the *Venus* had been sold for scrap and replaced by the second-hand *Lancelot* (1868). In 1877, too, the *Largs* was sold off the Clyde.

With the fleet thus denuded of two workhorses, some replacement was desperately needed, the more so as the rival G&SW Railway had opened their new Glasgow St Enoch terminus. This was conveniently situated on the north bank of the river, and traffic for Rothesay was being won back, despite the steamer leg of the total journey being much longer. In the flier *Sultana* (1868), owned by Captain Alex Williamson but connecting with the Sou'West trains at Greenock (Prince's Pier), Gillies & Campbell had a formidable rival. The new steamer which appeared in 1877 came from the Caird stable and was named *Sheila*, faster, heavier and better furnished than the older steamers. She was put on the packet runs in the morning and evening and sailed from and to Port Bannatyne, Rothesay and the newly-opened pier at the fashionable suburb of Craigmore where those enjoying their summer residences away from the city would board. A new faster train service was inaugurated, leaving Glasgow (Bridge Street) at 1635 (half an hour later than the 1605 from St Enoch) and calling only at Port Glasgow for the collection of tickets. No luggage was allowed. Rothesay for the first time was brought within ninety minutes of the centre of the city. (From 1878, the *Sheila* sailed to Arran in the middle of the day.) The rivalry between the *Sheila* and *Sultana* was legendary and took place at white heat, especially in the race for Craigmore Pier in the evening. It was left to lesser vessels to call at the piers at Innellan and Toward.

The final addition to the fleet in the seventies was the *Adela* (1877), another unremarkable, unglamorous but dependable paddler, again from Caird's. She inherited the engines of the ill-fated *Lady Gertrude*.

An image of Rothesay Harbour between 1866 and 1876 with the Wemyss Bay
steamer *Largs* berthed along the end and Hutcheson's *Iona* in the middle berth
of the outer pier   G W Wilson & Co., Aberdeen

A further image of Rothesay Habour, in 1876; the *Lady Gertrude* and *Athole* occupy
the inner berth while the *Argyle* (closer) and *Marquis of Bute* are moored outside
                                                                    G W Wilson & Co., Aberdeen

The withdrawal from the Gillies & Campbell fleet of their flagship *Sheila* came quicker than one might have anticipated. Perhaps she had lost some of her speed in the early eighties; perhaps she ate up too much coal. It appears that in September 1881 she was offered for sale but her actual demise came about differently. Her master, Captain Duncan Bell, and the master of MacBrayne's great Royal Mail steamer *Columba*, Captain John McGaw, were not exactly the best of friends. As the *Sheila* headed from Wemyss Bay to Innellan on the 9th of the month the *Columba* appeared round Toward Point. Determined to reach the pier first, Bell approached from an unusual direction, having ignored the long blast on the *Columba's* whistle as she too approached the pier. The *Sheila* did actually 'win' but the *Columba* was unable to stop and her stem sliced through her plates below the water line. Prompt action saved any injuries, and the *Sheila* was able to be towed to Greenock for repair. While on the slip, she was sold out of the fleet.

The *Sheila* was replaced by the more economical but less reliable *Bonnie Doon* (1876), a steamer which had spent some time on the Thames after being built for the Glasgow-Ayr traffic. The fleet was further augmented by the purchase in 1884 of the distinctly old-fashioned *Dunoon Castle* (1867). Renamed *Arran*, she was kept away from the limelight carrying out freight runs and subsidiary services. At the other end of the spectrum came the *Victoria* in June 1886. She was the last ship to be added to the fleet and was a direct replacement for the *Bonnie Doon*. Of the same high standard of elegance, comfort and speed as the flagships of the rival fleets on the Firth, she did much to restore the fortunes of Captain Campbell. Like the *Sheila* before her, she was used on the busy commuter runs to and from Rothesay and acted as an excursion steamer during the day.

Estrangement between Railway and Steamers

Relationships between the Directors of the Wemyss Bay Railway, the parent Caledonian and the steamboat owners, latterly the younger Captain Campbell on his own, were often fraught. The first serious rift came on 31 December 1881. Negotiations were proceeding regarding the division of through fares between Glasgow and the coast resorts, the railway directors believing that Campbell was taking too high a

A rare deck view of the Wemyss Bay steamer *Adela* while alongside at Rothesay, the steering wheel on the promenade deck being particularly prominent

The old meets the new: the two-funnelled Wemyss Bay steamer *Victoria* and the new CSP steamer from Gourock, the *Caledonia*, leave Rothesay, with the new pier buildings, in 1889

Francis Frith

proportion of the revenue. Matters came to a head that Hogmanay when Campbell simply withdrew his vessels and left the Wemyss Bay trains without any steamer connections. This *impasse* continued for over ten weeks. The Brandanes did not really suffer as they were still served from the Upper Firth by All the Way steamers and those connecting not just with the G&SW trains but also with those belonging to the North British Railway feeding into Helensburgh on the North Bank of the river. The Caledonian directors, however, fearing permanent loss of revenue from the boat trains, intervened and caused both sides eventually to come to an agreement. The Wemyss Bay directors had been on the verge of an arrangement with Captain Williamson to provide a service but the parent company found these proposals unacceptable. Full service was resumed on 22 March.

The Wemyss Bay Railway Company continued to be dissatisfied with the service of Captain Campbell, maintaining that his steamers were "insufficient". The railwaymen had a certain justification as the ships were known to break down fairly frequently, or run late, causing disruption to the train service. Another cause of disharmony was the fact that the new *Victoria* was very popular and was frequently used for lucrative charters, thus removing her from the 'bread and butter' railway connection work. The directors even managed to forge an agreement with David MacBrayne himself to work the connecting services, but once again the mighty Caledonian intervened and refused permission.

Captain Alex Campbell's lack of cooperation with his railway partners continued unabated and even the Caledonian directors, previously allied with him, became displeased. Events of a profound nature, however, hastened the demise of the old company.

Caledonian Takeover

The Caledonian Railway, having smarted at the lion's share of the Dunoon and Rothesay traffic going to the Glasgow & South Western via Greenock (Prince's Pier), purchased Gourock harbour, excavated a tunnel west from their terminus in Greenock, used the excavations to infill part of Gourock Bay and extended their railway line to a new wooden steamboat wharf half a mile long on the west shore. The new

Caley takeover: the new *Marchioness of Bute* berths at Wemyss Bay in the 1890s, before the building of the new station

Excursionists aboard the paddle steamer *Ivanhoe* returning from a day cruise in time for the evening express service from Wemyss Bay in the late 1890s

railhead at Gourock was opened on 1 June 1889: this event proved to be a watershed in Clyde steamer history. Meanwhile, after being refused Parliamentary permission to run their own steamers, the directors resorted to forming a private limited company, The Caledonian Steam Packet Company (CSP), to do so.

In the autumn of 1889, the shareholders of the Wemyss Bay Railway, realising that, with traffic falling, they could not compete with the new Gourock route, sold out to the Caledonian Railway and so Caledonian directors took over the running of the company. Meanwhile the CSP, under their enterprising and astute Marine Superintendent Captain James Williamson, ordered two new paddle steamers to be built in Port Glasgow, essentially for service at Wemyss Bay. Captain Alex Campbell tried to sell his ageing fleet but the CSP did not play ball. Being conscious that the game was essentially over, he gave notice on 22 April 1890 that he intended to withdraw from the Wemyss Bay route at the end of the month. This was just what the Caledonian wanted to hear and so they did nothing to stop him. On 1 May the sailings continued uninterrupted but in place of the *Adela* and *Lancelot* were two CSP vessels, Rothesay being served by the two-funnelled flagship *Galatea* (1889). A new era had begun. A further momentous improvement occurred on the same day when the Glasgow terminal was switched from the old Bridge Street station, south of the Clyde and well away from the commercial heart of the city, to the modern and convenient Central Station. Traffic started to return. The *Galatea* was employed rather as the *Sheila* and *Victoria* had been, namely on the busy packet sailings morning and evening and on excursions during the day. The daytime sailings to and from Rothesay were undertaken from the end of May largely by one of the new 1890 paddlers, the *Marchioness of Breadalbane*. The all yellow funnel and dark blue hull of the new had replaced the stark black and white of the old steamers. In 1893 the Caledonian actually absorbed the Greenock & Wemyss Bay Railway Company and the transition was complete.

During the 1890s, often referred to as the 'high noon' of the Clyde paddle steamer, competition was at white heat, especially between the Caley and their main rivals, the Sou'West. Starting in 1892, the latter had built a fleet of crack steamers, arguably superior to the new CSP

The Caley flagship *Galatea* (right) alongside the middle berth at Rothesay with MacBrayne's flagship *Columba* trying to berth at the concave west end around 1894

Two CSP paddlers at Rothesay Pier in the last stages of reconstruction in 1899: the *Duchess of Rothesay* arriving and the *Marchioness of Breadalbane* alongside boats, and the races which took place especially on Monday mornings and Saturday afternoons were legendary. The fastest route to and from Rothesay was still by Wemyss Bay and so the Caledonian held on to a fair share of the traffic, most of the intense competition being between the adversaries at Gourock and Prince's Pier. The ships employed at Wemyss Bay were not the fastest or the most lavishly furnished. The sister of the *Marchioness of Breadalbane*, the *Marchioness of Bute*, soon joined her at Wemyss Bay while the *Galatea* was transferred elsewhere. The third 'Marchioness' in the fleet, the *Marchioness of Lorne* (1890) was also found at Wemyss Bay, as initially was the paddler *Caledonia* (1889). Largs and Millport were served in addition, and the complicated rosters which evolved meant that one vessel was not exclusively on the Rothesay-Wemyss Bay route but took in other destinations and at some point of the day even sailed out of Gourock.

Upgrading

In 1884 new brick buildings on Rothesay Pier replaced the old wooden ones. It was from this period that the landmark central clock tower with small baronial turrets at each corner dated. About ten years later, with the massive upsurge in traffic caused by the competition among the railway companies and between them and the private owners, the pier itself was proving inadequate, especially troublesome being the concave west berth. Legal arguments took a great deal of time to resolve, but eventually, in July 1899, the reconstruction work was complete and Rothesay could boast a three berth wooden pier, both the length and the breadth being substantially increased. The structure remained essentially the same for over sixty years.

On the Wemyss Bay line too there were huge improvements. The Caley had been operating the single, steeply graded line with great difficulty, especially in summer when time was at a premium. Superior engines were employed from 1899 but that did not completely solve the problem. Eventually the decision was taken in the closing months of the century to double a fair proportion of the line between Port Glasgow and Wemyss Bay and to rebuild the station and pier at Wemyss Bay, at that time one of the least salubrious on the Firth. The first double section was complete by 1 June 1903 and the new station and pier opened on 7 December – the railhead now surpassing even Prince's Pier for

The rebuilding of Wemyss Bay station and pier in 1903, with the *Marchioness of Bute* alongside

Edwardian splendour: the interior of the newly reconstructed Wemyss Bay station in 1904-05

Edwardian splendour and elegance. The old station was widened and the new station buildings were dominated by a sixty-foot high clock tower. The pier was doubled in width and the passageway to and from the station covered with a glass roof. The stationmaster at the time was one William Robison and, as an expert gardener, he introduced tasteful floral decorations throughout the station and walkway.

The timetable was speeded up – it was now possible to travel between Glasgow and Rothesay in 75 minutes. In that 1903 summer six steamers from the ten active units in the CSP fleet were required at different times of the day to deliver the seven weekday scheduled sailings from Wemyss Bay to Craigmore, Rothesay and sometimes Port Bannatyne. Bringing the commuters in the morning were the *Marchioness of Lorne*, at 0610 and 0835 from Rothesay, with the splendid *Duchess of Rothesay* (1895) taking the busiest crossing at 0730 before she proceeded to Toward for a run up to Gourock. The first down run was the 0910 from Wemyss Bay, taken by the *"Breadalbane"*, shortly followed at 0925 on most days by the twin-funnelled cruise steamer *Ivanhoe* (1880), en route to Arran, Ailsa Craig, etc. The *"Rothesay"* was back at 1040, when she left for Rothesay and Arran via the Kyles, and she would pass the *"Breadalbane"* off Toward as she carried out her 1050 up run. When she reached Wemyss Bay, the *"Breadalbane"* carried on to Millport, while her sister, the *Marchioness of Bute*, arrived from Millport and then sailed to Rothesay (and then back to Millport via Kilchattan Bay). There was now a considerable gap in sailings, although Rothesay was of course still served from Gourock, Prince's Pier and Craigendoran (which was the North British railhead by this time). A further interchange of "Marchionesses" took place at Wemyss Bay at 1525. The cruising paddler *Duchess of Rothesay* sailed back from Rothesay at 1630 while the *Ivanhoe* took the 1730 ex Wemyss Bay in connection with the express train. A Rothesay-Wemyss Bay double run at 1835/1905 (a remarkably quick turnround) by the new crack steamer *Duchess of Fife* (1903) completed the day. The two "Marchionesses", incidentally changed rosters daily. On the appearance of the Caley's first turbine steamer *Duchess of Argyll* on the Arran route in 1906 the magnificent paddler *Duchess of Hamilton* (1890) was displaced and took over the excursion traffic from the *Ivanhoe*, thus becoming the main evening express steamer from Wemyss Bay to Rothesay.

The *Marchioness of Breadalbane* in the south berth at Wemyss Bay, with the notice 'Caledonian Railway' prominent above the station entrance

Satellite pier: the *Duchess of Rothesay* alongside the 1900 extension to Innellan pier with the old pierhead clearly seen in the foreground. The *Isle of Arran* approaches from the north

Services Pooled

It became obvious half way through the 1900s that the extravagant competition among the railway companies could not last. Dividends began to fall and shareholders became restless. Captain James Williamson of the CSP took action in 1907 by laying up one steamer, the *Ivanhoe*, and pruning unprofitable runs, while the following year he sold the *Marchioness of Bute* off the river. In 1909, however, the 'Clyde Coast Pool' took effect and, *inter alia*, the most wasteful competition ceased. Certain rival services were combined with one steamer servicing both company's railheads. The *Duchess of Hamilton* was placed on the Arran via Kyles roster, thus relegating the *Duchess of Rothesay* to more mundane railway connection work out of Wemyss Bay and Gourock. In this she partnered the *Duchess of Fife* and *Duchess of Montrose* (1902) for three years. The three paddle "Duchesses" therefore became the mainstay of the Rothesay service. By now the complex rosters including the circular route from Wemyss Bay to Rothesay, returning by Kilchattan Bay, Millport and Largs were a thing of the past. The *Marchioness of Breadalbane* spent some seasons largely on supplementary cargo runs before settling down as the main Millport-Wemyss Bay steamer. Wemyss Bay had seen calls by turbine steamers but not by the new Caley flagship *Duchess of Argyll* until 1911 when she was assigned the Arran via Kyles roster for one year, sailing via Rothesay in each direction.

The red and black funnels of the G&SW opposition were thus due to appear at the Caley strongholds. This did not happen at Wemyss Bay to any extent except in 1910 and 1912 when the handsome *Jupiter* (1896) and the mighty *Glen Sannox* (1892) respectively were allocated to the Arran via Kyles route, sailing in both directions via Wemyss Bay and Rothesay. In most years the *Duchess of Hamilton* was the general excursion steamer (including the main early evening Wemyss Bay-Rothesay run) but in 1911 the *Jupiter* undertook this duty. The 'ferry-class' Sou'West paddlers were generally kept away from Wemyss Bay. With minor variations, this pattern continued until the outbreak of war.

The Great War and After

Britain declared war on Germany on 4 August 1914. The Clyde steamer services carried on as normal until early in 1915, when some ships were

Satellite pier: one of the very rare images of a steamer at Toward Pier, the *Marchioness of Bute* arriving

Satellite pier: CSP flagship *Galatea* alongside the iron pier at Craigmore around 1900

requisitioned for war service. A Shipping Controller, under Admiralty restrictions, soon took over responsibility for a joint steamer service. It was realised that paddle steamers, with their shallow draft, made very good minesweepers and one by one nearly all the Clyde pleasure steamers left to serve under the white ensign. The CSP fared worst, as every single ship was taken over by the Admiralty. Two, the *Duchess of Hamilton* and *Duchess of Montrose*, were war losses while the *Marchioness of Lorne* never saw further service.

Operating the services became more difficult when, on 1 July 1915, the Cloch-Dunoon anti-submarine boom was erected and the Clyde partitioned. Rothesay, together with Innellan, Toward and Craigmore, was now totally reliant on Wemyss Bay. Two steamers were allocated purely to the Rothesay-Wemyss Bay service, the first time this had ever happened. Initially the *Duchess of Rothesay* was assisted by the *Caledonia*, the first time the latter had been regularly on the route. By 1916, however, the "*Rothesay*" had been called up and her place had been taken by the old *Ivanhoe*, back in the Caley fleet on charter. The *Caledonia* was now working above the boom and the *Marchioness of Breadalbane* appeared again at Wemyss Bay. The service was at this point supplemented by the great MacBrayne paddler *Columba* (1878), which now berthed at Rothesay and gave a public sailing morning and evening to and from Wemyss Bay before and after her sailing to the Kyles, Tarbert and Ardrishaig.

Matters got worse in 1917 when the last of the Caley paddlers were requisitioned and the company had to make do entirely with chartered tonnage. That season the main incumbent on the Rothesay run was MacBrayne's veteran *Iona* (1864), her funnels being even changed from red to yellow for a while. She was assisted if required by another West Highland steamer, the smaller *Fusilier* (1888), and possibly other refugees from the north, but in most instances she just had to struggle on on her own.

Hostilities ceased on 11 November 1918 but it was many months before the Clyde returned to normal, although the boom was dismantled in February 1919. Ships had to be brought home and then reconditioned, the repair yards being full to overflowing. Eventually the *Duchess of*

Satellite pier: children on the shore watching the Caley paddler *Duchess of Fife* leaving Port Bannatyne Pier in the 1900s

A fine shot of the *Duchess of Rothesay* arriving at Wemyss Bay in 1919, with the chartered MacBrayne steamer *Chevalier* in the Millport berth

Aerial Photos Ltd., Edinburgh

Argyll returned to service, on 31 May 1919, and replaced the *Fusilier* on the Rothesay-Wemyss Bay station, the first time a turbine steamer had appeared on this run. In July she revived the Arran via Kyles excursion, incorporating of course a Wemyss Bay-Rothesay crossing morning and afternoon. By now, the practice of combining Gourock-Dunoon and Wemyss Bay-Rothesay in the one roster had returned, the *Iona* and *Ivanhoe* being allocated to these duties. Switching on a daily basis, one served Rothesay in the morning and Dunoon in the afternoon, and *vice versa*.

1920 saw normality beginning to return, although the number of steamers was significantly reduced and, what with the horrendous loss of life, industrial unrest and inflation, the public's outlook on life had drastically changed since 1914. The old way of life had gone for ever. Between 1920 and 1923, the *Duchess of Rothesay* and *Duchess of Fife* alternated weekly on the Rothesay and Dunoon rosters. One was essentially thirled to Wemyss Bay with one sailing daily (in the early afternoon) to Dunoon and Gourock and the other worked most of the Gourock-Dunoon sailings with only an odd run from 'the Bay'. Some small piers also closed, with Toward receiving its final call in the spring of 1922.

Railway Grouping

Following on from the pooling agreement of 1909 and the fact that all Clyde steamer services were controlled jointly during the war, it seemed inevitable that some form of cooperation would continue in peacetime. The Railway Act of 1921 ensured this would happen and on 1 January 1923 the G&SW railway company was absorbed by the London Midland and Scottish Railway Company (LMS), the Caledonian Railway and the associated Caledonian Steam Packet Co becoming subsidiaries on 1 July. The steamers now controlled (ultimately from London) by the LMS had their funnels painted yellow with a red band and black top, but by 1925 a uniform yellow and black funnel was finally adopted.

Two significant changes to the Rothesay 'ferry' runs took place in 1923 as a result of the railway amalgamation. For the first time the roster of the former G&SW paddler *Mercury* (1892) was fully integrated with the

The LMS era: the former G&SW flier *Mercury* alongside Craigmore on 18 July 1928 while on the railway connection services

Leo Vogt

INTERIOR OF STATION, WEMYSS BAY.

The LMS era: Wemyss Bay's splendid walkway between station and pier taken in the 1930s; the floral decorations and the paddle crest of one of the withdrawn first-generation Caley paddle steamers are prominent

Valentine

CSP schedules. The *Mercury* took the important 0710 ex Rothesay and the 1815 ex Wemyss Bay, in both cases en route to or from Prince's Pier. During the day she continued on the age-old Midday Kyles run, but the Kyles were no longer the preserve solely of the Sou'West paddlers. The former CSP paddle steamer *Duchess of Rothesay* now usually lay at Kames Pier overnight and gave the morning and evening packet services, via Rothesay of course, to and from Wemyss Bay, and not, traditionally, to Prince's Pier. The "*Rothesay*", conversely, sailed to Dunoon, Gourock and Prince's Pier in the early afternoon while the *Duchess of Fife*, normally on the Gourock station, served Wemyss Bay. Meanwhile, the *Jupiter*, for some years on an excursion sailing from Greenock to Ayr, now called daily en route to Rothesay, on the outward journey, at Wemyss Bay. On the days she was not making for Ayr the morning run to Rothesay was largely used as a much-needed cargo run.

Following the 1926 season, when the General Strike caused the Clyde services to be pared to the absolute minimum, the *Duchess of Rothesay* and *Mercury* exchanged places. This was regarded as promotion for the "*Rothesay*" - she was now regarded as the smarter of the two ships, belying her age, and so was more suited to the prestigious Midday Kyles run. This distribution of vessels lasted for seven years, till the *Mercury* was withdrawn from service at the end of the 1933 season. From 1930, the new palatial cruising turbine *Duchess of Montrose*, with her enclosed promenade deck and single-class structure, incorporated Wemyss Bay-Rothesay crossings in her programme most days. Port Bannatyne Pier around this time got a new lease of life. After the Great War the railway steamers had not resumed calling and the pier became more and more decrepit. In 1933, however, the strenuous efforts of the piermaster and his MP brought about its renaissance and the steamers from Wemyss Bay and the other railheads began to berth once more.

A New Generation

Throughout the thirties, despite suffering from the aftermath of the Depression, the LMS/CSP continued to replace old tonnage with new, modern-looking ships far removed from the traditional Clyde paddle steamer. In 1934 came quasi-sisters, the *Caledonia* and *Mercury*, indirectly replacing the old paddlers of the same name. Their arrival

The LMS era: the new *Mercury* of 1934 approaching Port Bannatyne pier on 24 August 1936

Jim McCaul

The LMS era: the new *Juno* of 1937 at the Rothesay berth at Wemyss Bay on 8 September 1937

William Blackett

impinged on the Rothesay-Wemyss Bay narrative as the former took over from the *Jupiter* (though the Ayr run was discontinued) and so she took what was essentially a cargo run at 1030 from Wemyss Bay, while the latter replaced the *Duchess of Rothesay* on the Midday Kyles roster. The *"Rothesay"* was again demoted to railway connection work, once more partnering the *Duchess of Fife*. The two "Duchesses" now interchanged daily. The steamer which started off in the Kyles (now Auchenlochan as Kames Pier was closed in 1928) served Wemyss Bay in the morning, made her afternoon appearance at Gourock and covered the evening Wemyss Bay runs, berthing at Rothesay. Next day she would concentrate on Dunoon in the morning and Wemyss Bay in the afternoon ready to take the 1725 Wemyss Bay-Rothesay-Kyles, where she berthed overnight.

The next change occurred in 1936. The vessels of Turbine Steamers Ltd which ran day excursions to Campbeltown and Inveraray were bought by MacBrayne's to replace the ancient but well-loved *Columba* and *Iona*, which were withdrawn. The goodwill of the turbines' service passed to the CSP and the *Duchess of Argyll* replaced them. Her place on the Arran via Kyles roster was taken by the *Caledonia* while the *Mercury* superseded her on the afternoon cruise roster. The two new paddlers therefore continued to have an association with the Rothesay-Wemyss Bay station. The *Duchess of Rothesay* once more returned to the Midday Kyles run, the *"Fife"* now being partnered by a strange bedfellow, the *Queen-Empress*. This white-funnelled paddler had been part of the Williamson-Buchanan fleet sailing largely 'doon the watter' from Glasgow – the fleet had been taken over by the CSP.

The following year, 1937, saw two new modern second-generation paddle steamers being added to the CSP fleet, the *Jupiter* and *Juno*. They were both designed as workhorses and replaced the *Duchess of Fife* and the *Queen-Empress* on the basic Dunoon and Rothesay schedules, the older steamers being transferred to Millport. Although still very much associated with Wemyss Bay, the *"Fife"* relinquished her connection with Rothesay which had been unbroken for 33 years (at least in peacetime). She now berthed at the south berth at Wemyss Bay, the north, or right hand, berth being reserved for the Rothesay steamer. This arrangement continued until the outbreak of war.

The Second World War and After

Unlike in 1914, when war was declared on 3 September 1939, the change was instant. Many of the Clyde steamers were used for evacuation duties and as tenders to the troopships at the Tail of the Bank off Greenock. The anti-submarine boom from Cloch to Dunoon was quickly put in place and the Firth was once more divided in two. For three weeks the Rothesay-Wemyss Bay service was in the hands of the *Caledonia* but on 21 September she, like the other CSP paddlers, was requisitioned. The turbines remained and from then until the end of the war the *Duchess of Montrose* seldom deviated from the Wemyss Bay-Innellan-Rothesay station. She was relieved as required either by the *Duchess of Argyll* or the smaller turbine *Marchioness of Graham* (1936), in peacetime the second Arran steamer. As in the Great War, MacBrayne's Ardrishaig Mail Steamer had to operate from Wemyss Bay and lay overnight at Rothesay. For the first three months the three-funnelled turbine steamer *Saint Columba* (1912) was on the run but for most of the war the incumbent was the diesel electric motor vessel *Lochfyne* (1931). Throughout most of the conflict the ships were painted battleship grey, saloon windows were boarded up so that lights would not shine through and anti-aircraft steel wheelhouses were fitted. Rothesay's two satellite piers were soon closed – Port Bannatyne immediately and Craigmore in mid-October 1939. Neither was ever to re-open. The war caused Wemyss Bay pier to open for the first time on Sundays, three crossings being timetabled. Railway Sunday sailings had commenced on 6 June 1909 but all services to Rothesay were from the other railheads. Wemyss Bay had not been brought into use during the Great War (as might have been expected thanks to the boom) as Sunday sailings had ceased altogether and had not been reinstated until 1923. When peace returned, incidentally, the pier was closed once more on winter Sundays, traffic to Rothesay reverting to the Gourock route.

As in 1918 so in 1945. Although VE Day was celebrated on 8 May 1945 it was a year later when a degree of normality returned. Of the steamers associated with the Rothesay-Wemyss Bay service, two were war casualties, the *Mercury* and *Juno*. Both had served on the Firth for only a short time. The veteran *Duchess of Rothesay* was a mere hulk lying near

Harwich and could not be reconditioned. The fleet then was considerably smaller and also unbalanced, with more turbines and fewer paddlers than in an ideal world. Early in 1946 two of these turbines made their first appearance – in a relief capacity - on the Rothesay-Wemyss Bay roster, the *Duchess of Hamilton* (1932), sister of the *"Montrose"*, and the *King Edward* (1901), the first commercial turbine steamer ever built.

By the time the summer had arrived a curtailed service compared with 1939 had been put in place. The two remaining substantial LMS paddlers of the 1930s, *Caledonia* and *Jupiter*, were allocated to the basic Rothesay rosters – from Gourock as well as Wemyss Bay, the direct point-to-point sailings having ceased after the war ended and the boom dismantled. They now both lay at Rothesay overnight, the morning and evening runs from and to the Kyles being a thing of the past. The *Duchess of Argyll* was demoted to the Midday Kyles run (now lightly loaded and uneconomic), this roster initially including a call at Wemyss Bay on the return journey. 1946 was the last year of a daily Arran via Kyles sailing and the ship carrying out the roster, the *Duchess of Montrose*, thus appeared on the Wemyss Bay-Rothesay crossing. The pattern of the long day excursions from Gourock, in response to the fluctuating habits of the travelling public, changed from 1947, with the frequency of each cruise altering. The Campbeltown steamer, usually the *Duchess of Hamilton*, bypassed Wemyss Bay, while the turbine making for Inveraray or Arran via Kyles, usually the *Duchess of Montrose*, called before crossing to Rothesay. For the last two years of her life, 1950 and '51, the ageing *Duchess of Argyll* was relegated to ferry chores and partnered the *Jupiter* on the basic Rothesay services, while the *Caledonia* temporarily revived her prewar afternoon cruises.

Nationalisation

The reason that the *"Argyll"* could give up the age-old Midday Kyles run was that the rump of that service was taken over by one of the Craigendoran paddlers. The North Bank fleet, originally belonging to the North British but from 1923 the London and North Eastern Railway (LNER), had not impinged on the Rothesay-Wemyss Bay story. On 1 January 1948, however, the assets of all the country's railways were

The early days of World War II: relief turbine *Marchioness of Graham* (left), still retaining her CSP funnel, at Rothesay along with MacBrayne's *Loch Aline*, requisitioned as an examination vessel, on 2 January 1940   Leo Vogt

The final days of World War II: regular Rothesay-Wemyss Bay turbine *Duchess of Montrose*, with bomb-proof wheel house and looking the worse for wear, approaching Rothesay pier in June 1945

vested in a new state authority, The British Transport Commission, trading under the name 'British Railways'. Despite being erstwhile deadly rivals, the LMS and LNER fleets were forced together. True integration took several years to achieve, but the replacement of the *Duchess of Argyll* by the diesel electric paddle vessel *Talisman* on the morning run from Greenock (Princes Pier) was an early example of what could be achieved. An interesting innovation took place in 1949. With the general introduction of the five-day working week, traffic to Rothesay on Saturday mornings built up enormously. The two turbine steamers which sailed all the way from Glasgow (Bridge Wharf) to the coast now called at Wemyss Bay en route between Dunoon and Rothesay to relieve congestion. The commodious *Queen Mary II* (1933) called around 1300 and the *King Edward* an hour later.

The new nationalised Railway Executive did not have their problems to seek. Apart from the war losses and the resultant imbalance in the fleet, only the *Talisman* burned diesel fuel, all the other ships being reliant on ever scarcer, more expensive and poorer quality coal. Inflation, increased competition from road transport and changed holiday habits all militated against economic success, especially as the public refused to accept realistic fares increases. Perhaps the deadliest blow was the derationing of petrol in 1950 after which more and more people came to rely on the motor car and fewer and fewer on public transport.

The size of the Clyde steamer fleet was cut in 1952 by the withdrawal of two elderly turbine steamers, including the *Duchess of Argyll*, and cruising was pruned. The *Duchess of Hamilton* was the only regular rostered day excursion steamer from Gourock – she called daily at Wemyss Bay en route to Rothesay. Of more significance to the 'ferry' services, however, was the decision at last to do away with the criss-crossing of the firth and the introduction of a genuine point-to-point service between Rothesay and Wemyss Bay and Gourock-Dunoon. The *Caledonia* and *Jupiter* shared these duties and exchanged rosters weekly. Six crossings daily were given in each direction, but there were still three calls every weekday at Innellan. From this season, the *Duchess of Montrose* replaced the Bridge Wharf turbines on the Saturday morning relief sailings.

Crack turbine steamer *Duchess of Hamilton*, dressed overall, pulls away from Rothesay in 1948

Cargo and milk churns at the after end of the turbine *Duchess of Argyll* as she nears Wemyss Bay while on 'ferry chores' on 21 July 1950

Geoffrey Grimshaw

A Third Generation – The Coming of the Diesel

It was in February 1951 that a momentous announcement was made. A million pounds was to be spent by BR on modernising the Clyde fleet. The new ships were all to have diesel rather than steam engines. Four smallish passenger ships were to appear in 1953 and three 'dual-purpose vessels' which could handle vehicles and cargo at all states of the tide a year later. The idea of car ferries on the Firth had been mooted in the thirties and plans had been drawn up – but the war intervened. Wemyss Bay-Rothesay did not normally feature in the schedules of the new passenger vessels, called "Maids", but the *Maid of Skelmorlie* introduced separate crossings to and from Innellan, thus streamlining the work of the Rothesay paddler.

The real revolution came on 4 January 1954 when the first of the 'car ferries', the *Arran*, commenced sailing between Gourock and Dunoon. She was joined at Easter by the second of the trio, the *Cowal*, and the vehicular traffic exceeded all expectations. That summer the *Jupiter* looked after Rothesay-Wemyss Bay on her own, although with there no longer being an early morning boat to Gourock the *Maid of Skelmorlie* now had to supplement some of the paddler's sailings.

The car ferry service between Rothesay and Wemyss Bay was inaugurated on 1 October 1954, by the *Cowal*. The chairman of the Scottish Tourist Board, the Rt Hon Thomas Johnston, performed the tape-cutting ceremony as the ship tied up at Rothesay for the first time. The new ferries were equipped with an electric hoist aft which could be raised and lowered between pier and car deck to suit all states of the tide. No longer did drivers have 'to drive the plank', totally unprotected against accidents, and only at suitable tides. The *Cowal* could accommodate 26 cars but her passenger capacity was only 650, half that of the paddle steamer she was replacing. The third car ferry, appropriately named *Bute*, took over from the *Cowal* on 6 December 1954; she was to settle down on the Rothesay-Wemyss Bay station for some years. The car ferries were an instant and phenomenal success, helped no doubt by the brilliant weather of the 1955 summer. Their coming coincided with the overt revival of The Caledonian Steam Packet Company – flags and the motif on seamen's jerseys testified to this welcome change.

A typical postwar scene at Rothesay, with the *Duchess of Montrose* at Berth 3 boarding for her day excursion sailing while the paddle steamer *Caledonia* casts off for Wemyss Bay around 1950   Photo chrom

An early photo of the pioneer car ferry *Arran*, sporting her original goalpost mainmast, alongside Rothesay in the mid-1950s

Because the *Bute* was hoist-loading, a fair amount of time had to be given at each pier for her to turn round, with the result that she was only able to carry out six double runs per day (seven on Saturdays). The timetable remained static for several years, departures from Rothesay being (SX) at 0645, 0845, 1045, 1330, 1645 and 1945, returning from Wemyss Bay at 0745, 0945, 1200, 1510, 1820 and 2035. A two-hour interval service was offered on Saturdays and Sundays. The charge for "accompanied Motor Cars at owner's risk" was 22/- (£1.10) for a single journey and 33/- (£1.65) for a return for a car up to 12 h.p., more powerful cars being 25% more. Previously cars had been charged by weight. From 1958 it was considered more suitable to charge by length. A "Circular Tour" using the Gourock-Dunoon ferry one way was also offered.

Compared with the traditional Clyde steamer, the new diesels with their bus-like seats, cramped tearooms and noticeable vibration did draw negative comments, but they were warm, reliable and, most importantly, economical. The paddle steamer *Jupiter* was retained for three years as a passenger backup, especially at weekends, and she managed to reintroduce a form of Cumbrae Circle cruise on weekday afternoons. One class of traditional steamer, was, however, withdrawn immediately. On 1 October 1954 the cargo boat *Minard* gave her last run with heavy goods and freight from Glasgow to Rothesay. She was the last in a long line of vessels which had served Rothesay in this way – four of her predecessors had been named *Bute* – but the car ferry had made her and her way of life redundant. Now containers were loaded at Glasgow, sent down to the coast by rail and transferred on to the car deck of the Rothesay ferry by bogey. Originally the dual-purpose vessels had been given 'goalpost' masts and derricks for heaving on board and then stowing such cargo in an open hatch aft, but the facilities were quickly redundant, as it had been found more convenient to load the containers using the hoist. From 1959 the ferries appeared with a single tripod mainmast and with their after deck plated over. This had the added advantage of increasing car capacity from 26 to 34. Incidentally, when the lines to the coast were electrified in the sixties goods traffic had to come by road rather than rail.

Rothesay's own car ferry, MV *Bute*, calling at Innellan in the late 1950s

F G MacHaffie

Passengers, wrapped up against the cold, disembarking from the *Maid of Argyll* in the late 1950s

British Railways

The Final Years of Railway Control

A new car ferry appeared in 1957. This was the *Glen Sannox* and she was commissioned on the Arran service. One result of this was that Millport had to be serviced from Wemyss Bay by one of the 'ABC' ferries as far as cargo and vehicles were concerned. With three upper firth car ferries in commission that was not a problem, but in winter, when there were only two, time had to be taken from the Rothesay service to fulfil this need. From the summer of 1958 the three ABC ferries exchanged rosters on the Rothesay, Dunoon and 'Millport cargo' runs in an *ad hoc* fashion: from 1962 this rotation was regularised. One of the three spent the entire week on the Rothesay station and then spent two weeks either at Dunoon, Millport or on relief sailings.

1958 was the first year Rothesay had to cope without the *Jupiter*. The much smaller *Maid of Skelmorlie* took over her roster but as she could not cope on Saturdays she changed places with the last paddle steamer ever to be built for Clyde service – the *Waverley* (1947). She normally sailed out of Craigendoran. A second Craigendoran paddle steamer, the *Jeanie Deans*, exchanged schedules with the *Waverley* between 1961 and her withdrawal in 1964. The third paddler from the same stable, the *Talisman*, had become the Millport-Wemyss Bay steamer, and from 1958 until her withdrawal in 1967, she gave the last run of the day on Saturdays from Wemyss Bay to Rothesay.

Inflation, operating costs, changing holiday habits and poor weather all conspired to give the CSP a particularly bruising time in 1962. The company's loss escalated and action had to be taken. Eventually, in the midst of the Beeching cuts on the railways, the axe fell after the 1964 season and two major ships were withdrawn, not just the *Jeanie Deans* but also the favourite turbine *Duchess of Montrose*. The result was a revamping of the remaining rosters. A large paddler was no longer available to substitute for a "Maid" on the Saturday passenger back-up between Wemyss Bay and Rothesay. The only sizeable vessel to offer help was the turbine *Queen Mary II*, painted in the new CSP colour scheme with monastral blue hull and a red rampant lion on the funnel. She took over the mantle of the "*Montrose*" and so sailed over in a relief capacity around noon.

A typical summer Saturday morning at Rothesay around 1960 with the car ferry *Bute* arriving from Wemyss Bay, the small motor vessel *Countess of Breadalbane* (closest) connecting from Tighnabruaich and the turbine *Duchess of Hamilton* ready to sail to Campbeltown

Judges Ltd of Hastings

Pushing the pram on the prom at Rothesay oblivious to the *Maid of Argyll* (left) and *Arran* at the pier in the early 1960s

Caledonian Steam Packet Co.

The *Maid of Argyll* manoeuvring in a heavy swell at high tide at Rothesay on 19 April 1965

Geoffrey Grimshaw

A Saturday morning at Wemyss Bay: the car ferry *Glen Sannox* (right) ready to load cars while relief turbine *Queen Mary II* is at the head of the pier awaiting train passengers on July 10 1971

R B Boyd

The *Bute* shows her versatility as she unloads passengers, a flat of PLA (passengers' luggage in advance), a container, a motor cycle and a car at Wemyss Bay around 1959
British Railways

The *Glen Sannox* drafted in to convey a heavy load to Wemyss Bay from Rothesay on 12 December 1963

Caledonian Steam Packet Co.

1962 had a further significance for Rothesay. On 19 May a disastrous fire gutted the pier buildings and consumed the much-loved Victorian clock tower. The edifice had to be demolished to first floor level. Against the odds, however, Rothesay Harbour Trust built a two storey building to house offices, waiting room and all the other ancillary requirements of a modern terminal. The new structure was finally opened – by no less a personage than HM the Queen Mother - on 11 May 1968.

The Scottish Transport Group

1 January 1969 was a momentous year for the CSP. Thanks to the Transport Act of 1968, the company became a subsidiary of a new concern, the Scottish Transport Group, along with the Scottish Bus Group. After eighty years, the company was no longer under railway control. Senior Management came from the bus company and there was naturally a certain apprehension over the direction events might take. From July of that year the STG also assumed control of David MacBrayne Ltd, operating not only between Gourock and Ardrishaig but more importantly in the Western Isles. It became increasingly obvious that an amalgamation between the CSP and MacBrayne's, now under the same umbrella, was inevitable. It happened at last on 1 January 1973, when The Caledonian Steam Packet Company was renamed Caledonian MacBrayne Ltd., having taken over most of the shipping services of David MacBrayne Ltd. Through time, the 'new' company became popularly known as CalMac.

In the late sixties studies had been carried out on the possibility of two new large hoist-loading car ferries for the Clyde but the ideas were still-born. Instead the STG, on taking over, realised that the only way of eliminating the inevitable delays that occurred with that type of operation as traffic levels inexorably increased was to convert to drive-through operation. This would be expensive as not just would new tonnage with bow and stern ramps have to be built but new terminals fitted with linkspans would also have to be constructed. Rothesay Harbour Trust understandably balked at the idea. The STG themselves could call on the considerable resources of the Scottish Bus Group.

The world's last sea-going paddler *Waverley* at Wemyss Bay during her one year as a member of the Caledonian MacBrayne fleet, 1973

L J McDuff

CalMac hoist-loading ferry *Cowal* at Rothesay in 1974 before the days of roll-on roll-off; the *Bute* is behind her in Berth 1

J Aikman Smith

Momentous changes to the Clyde steamer and ferry scene took place in the first years of the seventies as a result of the new approach. In the case of Rothesay-Wemyss Bay, the consequence was that a larger ferry was allocated to the station. The first route to be converted to roll-on roll-off, as the practice became known, was Ardrossan-Brodick and this made the *Glen Sannox* redundant. Modified and fitted with a stern ramp so that she could in fact relieve on her original route, the "*Sannox*" was duly transferred to Rothesay, her first appearance on the Wemyss Bay roster being on 30 May 1970. She remained on the route full-time and, with her capacity for 1100 (compared with the previous 650), the need for a passenger relief evaporated. On Saturday mornings, however, the *Queen Mary II*, though employed very differently from before, still managed her relief sailing and a "*Maid*" still covered the busy 0745/1730 commuter runs, though no longer in winter. Because of her considerably greater height than the ABC ferries, a wooden ramp and then a gangway platform had to be constructed for the "*Sannox*" on Rothesay Pier. The provision of slipways at Largs and Cumbrae and the commissioning of two small bow-loading ferries meant that an 'ABC' class no longer had to cater for Millport. Though tangential to the main theme, it is of interest that on 23 December 1969 the CSP bought over the Bute Ferry Company, owned by the Marquess of Bute. This small concern provided a dual-purpose link across the Kyle of Bute between Rhubodach and Colintraive. Incremental improvements took place over the years, with bigger and better double-ended ferries being employed on the station.

The *Glen Sannox* only lasted eighteen months before she was transferred to Dunoon. Her last sailing was on 3 November 1971. The faithful *Bute* and *Cowal*, which had both found alternative employment on the Firth in 1970, returned to the fold. Between them they offered up to fourteen return crossings daily between Rothesay and Wemyss Bay, except on Sundays, when a two-hour interval service sufficed. One ferry coped on her own in winter.

In 1973, following the amalgamation of the Clyde and West Highland fleets, all the ships eventually had their funnels repainted – MacBrayne red with black top with a yellow circle sporting a Caledonian lion. This year saw the withdrawal of the *Waverley*, by now the last surviving

A deck view of the *Glen Sannox* nearing Wemyss Bay with the *Cowal* already at the pier on 12 October 1974

L J MacDuff

A view of the wharf at McAlpine's Ardyne yard around 1976; the *Glen Sannox*, from Wemyss Bay, shares the berth with the *Bournemouth Queen*, from Rothesay, and the *Sound of Islay*, on freight duty

W J H Bowie

paddle steamer, although it is well known that she was sold for a pound to the Paddle Steamer Preservation Society and still adorns the Firth today. Crossings by the excursion steamers had gradually been whittled down through the years of change. The turbine steamer *Queen Mary II* was the sole survivor and she herself bowed out gracefully after the 1977 season.

A significant feature of the mid-seventies was the commissioning of a new oil platform construction yard at Ardyne, just opposite Rothesay in Cowal, owned by Sir Robert McAlpine & Co. Large numbers of workers had to be transported there on a daily basis. Innellan pier, which had recently closed, was reopened between March and October 1974 but after that date new facilities at the Ardyne yard were brought into use. The Rothesay car ferries were largely responsible for the new service and inevitably the frequency between Rothesay and Wemyss Bay suffered. For a few weeks at the start of the exercise, certain runs were actually rerouted via Innellan.

A corollary of the formation of Caledonian MacBrayne was that ferries could now be employed either on the Clyde or in the West Highlands. The *Glen Sannox*, for example, spent the 1974 season as the Oban-Mull ferry but new tonnage displaced her and in 1975 she returned to the Clyde. This was fortuitous as the Ardyne workforce had increased enormously and a vessel of her capacity was required. She in fact replaced the *Bute*, which in turn, after receiving extended lift supports to cope with the huge tidal range at Mallaig, became the Skye ferry, at least in summer. In 1975, then, Rothesay was served by the *Cowal*, with the *Glen Sannox* sailing when she was available, and certainly on Saturdays.

A Second Car Ferry Generation

One of the last acts of the old CSP was to order from Lamont's of Port Glasgow two novel car ferries to be propelled unconventionally by Voith-Schneider units fore and aft to give maximum manoeuvrability. By now the terminals at both Gourock and Dunoon had been fitted with linkspans, the latter at right angles to the face of the pier, and the first of a new generation of car ferries, the *Jupiter*, was ready for service on that route in March 1974. She had a stern ramp for use at Gourock and a side ramp for Dunoon. She was joined by her sister, happily named *Juno*, the following December.

Talks had been going on for some time about a similar provision for Rothesay and Wemyss Bay. It was 26 May 1976 before the Government finally committed itself to spending £2.2m on new terminals – the last major Clyde piers to be converted - and a new "Jupiter class" vessel. Wemyss Bay, which had caused most problems because of the exposed nature of the site, was to have an end-loading linkspan installed at the south (formerly Millport) berth and Rothesay, in the interests of economy, a side-loading ramp at the middle berth of the pier. They were duly in place for the early summer of 1977, but sadly a serious fire had broken out at Wemyss Bay on 1 March of that year, causing extensive damage to the covered walkway between station and pier. Because of delays due to its listed building status, temporary passenger access and staff accommodation had to be installed.

The Wemyss Bay ramp was ready first, and was handselled on 20 May, Rothesay following on 4 June. In each case the vessel involved was the *Glen Sannox*, no longer required at Ardyne as the contract sailings there had ceased, coincidentally also in May, as the yard had failed to maintain a full order book. She had just received a very substantial overhaul and refurbishment to fit her for a possible life as a cruise 'steamer'. Meanwhile, the steadfast *Cowal*, the last of the ABCs in regular Clyde service, could not operate under the new system and was withdrawn. By a strange quirk of fate, her one-time sister *Arran* was available in her role as spare vessel to take up the secondary roster on Saturdays, the only day with more than a single-ship service, using the new terminals for the rest of that summer. She had been transferred to the Islay route in 1970 and had since been converted to stern-loading. She continued to appear from time to time until her own withdrawal in 1979. The "*Sannox*" was called away fairly frequently that summer, her place being taken by one of the new Dunoon ferries, mainly the *Jupiter*. Both the *Jupiter* and *Juno* were also employed transporting gas tankers to Rothesay from Gourock, landing them at the inner berth at the west end of the pier, which had been modified for use by a stern-loader as early as 1971.

Most importantly, the provision of ro-ro facilities greatly reduced loading time – to fifteen minutes - and a more than adequate service maintained by one vessel. Eight double runs were on offer each weekday, from Rothesay at 0645, 0900, 1100, 1300, 1430, 1600, 1730 and 1930, returning from Wemyss Bay at 0745, 1000, 1200, 1345, 1515, 1645, 1815 and 2030. Two years on, later sailings started to appear in the timetable for Friday and Saturday evenings.

A New Rothesay Ferry

The new ship promised for the route was launched from the Ailsa yard in Troon on 30 June 1977 but because of trouble with the alignment of her shafts her entry into service was delayed until early the following year. With ROTHESAY FERRY emblazoned on her side, the *Saturn* gave her maiden voyage on 2 February. She was a quasi-sister of the Dunoon pair, but more aesthetically pleasing, being fitted with a conventional high-level bridge and a tripod mainmast at the after end of the upper deck rather than the cumbersome arrangement in the earlier ships. Passenger accommodation was forward on two decks, the upper saloon doubling as a cafeteria, and there was ample open space on the upper deck, pleasingly finished in wood. The *Glen Sannox* now commenced a dual role as cruise ship cum car ferry. Not unlike the original paddlers operating out of Wemyss Bay in the nineteenth century, she was available on the ferry crossing at busy times, especially Saturday mornings, but could offer excursions on other days, thus replacing the Clyde's last turbine steamer. This arrangement, though sensible economically, did not work out in practice and after four seasons she was relegated to the status of spare vessel in summer, though still operating out of Oban in winter. With no 'inter-resort' working, Rothesay's connections were now solely with Wemyss Bay.

The eighties saw a gradual increase in traffic on the Rothesay station and, with CalMac facing political interference and increasing competition on the Dunoon run from a private concern, Western Ferries, the Rothesay-Wemyss Bay route eventually became the busiest in the whole network on a year-round basis.

The *Saturn*, initially the least reliable mechanically of the 'streakers', as the new ferries were affectionately called, suffered a major breakdown in 1982 and the *Glen Sannox* returned to Rothesay for a large part of the

GOUROCK-DUNOON ferry *Jupiter* loading at the new Rothesay linkspan on 18 September 1977

The launch of Rothesay's own second generation car ferry *Saturn* from the Ailsa yard in Troon on 30 June 1977

J Aikman Smith

summer. At this time, by Government decree, CalMac's Dunoon service was restricted to an hourly frequency, and the *Jupiter*, after spending most of the 1981 season laid up, was now available for other duties. When not needed to fulfil an RNAD contract between Gourock and Kilcreggan, she was able to offer much-needed assistance at Rothesay. Her schedule was known as the '1A Roster' and this came to involve an additional double run in summer between Wemyss Bay and Rothesay around 0940 on weekdays and extra help on an *ad hoc* basis in the mid-afternoon. This run was given on an all-year-round basis from winter 1987/88. With the *Glen Sannox* now laid up and only brought out to assist on special occasions like Bute and Cowal Games in late August, her mantle as the second Saturday ferry fell naturally to the *Jupiter*. Another vessel which was to become closely associated with Rothesay put in an appearance for the first time at Easter 1980. This was the former Islay ferry *Pioneer* (1974), now employed as the summer Mallaig-Armadale ferry (in place of the *Bute*) and so available for other duties in the off-season.

Perhaps as an indication that a rota was going to be set up, the legends on the hulls of the streakers were painted out during their overhauls in the winter of 1982/83. With the *Saturn* continuing to be dogged by technical problems, she and the *Juno* exchanged places in early 1986, to allow the former to take up the less demanding 1A Roster. From 11 May on, however, the three 'Jupiter' class ferries rotated on a monthly basis. The *Glen Sannox* gave her final sailing on the Rothesay route on 14 September 1988; being no longer required at Oban in winter, she was taken out of service the following June and sold. The *Pioneer*, which had been the streakers' regular relief since 1987, became spare vessel. With there being no longer any need for a hoist in her new employment, it was removed and replaced by side ramps.

Further Improvements

Around this time both terminals received a fair amount of renovation. Major work took place at the crumbling edifice which was Wemyss Bay pier during 1987. It had been quite inadequate especially in stormy weather with the result that diversions to the more sheltered terminal at Gourock had been commonplace. The linkspan had to be closed for

The new ROTHESAY FERRY *Saturn* loading at the Wemyss Bay linkspan during her first month in service, 11 Febuary 1978

J Aikman Smith

Looking over the car deck on the *Jupiter* as she draws away from the Wemyss Bay linkspan on 17 April 1992

essential maintenance for three weeks in October 1990, car traffic being diverted to Gourock. [The same happened in July 2000.] Rothesay's turn came in 1989. Foundation settlement had been discovered in the pier buildings opened twenty years before and they were demolished. In place of the convex curve on the face of the pier a section was provided which was wider than before, to allow for future use of end-loading ferries. It incorporated precast concrete sponsons higher than any likely water, so that ships could berth at all states of the tide. This part of the reconstruction was complete by September 1990. The second phase started the following May and comprised rebuilding the pier's west arm and providing a 'roundhead' at the end to allow ships to turn. In addition the east end was upgraded and new pier buildings constructed. The complete works were officially opened on 1 May 1992. Finally, on 25 March 1994, the Grade A listed Wemyss Bay station was officially reopened by the Chairman of British Railways Board. It had been lovingly restored to its pristine Edwardian grandeur using original materials, like the timber sarking, wherever possible. Otherwise old had been replaced by new with similar constituents.

Now under the direct ownership of the Secretary of State for Scotland rather than the STG, CalMac continued to expand the Rothesay service in the nineties. The streakers were internally refurbished during the 1992/93 winter and the No 1A Roster was expanded to include extra sailings, especially on Fridays. The most radical change, however, came in 1994. Four vessels were now allocated to the Upper Clyde services, the *Pioneer* being returned to fulltime duties. She was based at Rothesay and undertook a secondary roster, while on two days per week, with a streaker covering for her, she introduced an inter-island excursion (with cars) from Rothesay to Brodick. Never attracting a great deal of traffic, this particular experiment was withdrawn after the 1998 season. On certain other days, a streaker reintroduced Clyde cruising around the middle of the day to the Kyles of Bute, vehicles being carried on the 'ferry part' of the voyage. During the brilliant summer of 1995, this popular innovation continued largely unchanged, with the streakers exhanging rosters on a fortnightly rather than a monthly basis. On 13 October that year, Kilcreggan pier received its last call from a CalMac vessel and so the time was ripe for a further extension of the Rothesay sector of the No 1A Roster, especially in the busy teatime period. Thus

In 1994 Rothesay had a two-ship service to Wemyss Bay; here the secondary vessel *Pioneer* approaches the linkspan, the wide section of the pier being clearly visible

The West Highland vessel *Claymore* pulls away from Rothesay after hoist-loading during linkspan repairs; the *Saturn* is arriving with passengers from Wemyss Bay on 15 November 1994

even in winter, with only three vessels in service, Rothesay now had the services of two ferries for a reasonable part of each day.

1996 and '97 were the peak years of the revival of CalMac cruising on the Firth. Excursions were now given daily, except Saturdays. The streakers, where vending machines had replaced the cafeteria service for economic reasons from December 1995, had their traditional catering restored six months later, albeit franchised out (till late 2004, when CalMac resumed control). Since 1994 they had been sailing with liferafts, together with an inflatable rescue boat to starboard, instead of conventional lifeboats.

A double whammy occurred in the early summer of 1998. A new vessel for the Western Isles, the *Clansman*, was unable to appear until July, with the result that the *Pioneer* was allocated her old Skye timetable. All Clyde cruising ceased and Rothesay was now served as in winter, with the '1A boat' coming down to Wemyss Bay when she was not required during peak periods at Dunoon. The former Skye ferry *Loch Dunvegan* attempted to keep the remainder of the service going on a passenger only basis until the second disaster struck. A serious breakdown occurred in the Western Isles and the "*Dunvegan*" too was required to fill in for a month. The passenger runs just had to be cancelled. Two streakers, however, were retained at Rothesay in the late afternoon as it was decided that the Dunoon commitment could be entrusted to a chartered vessel on a passenger only basis. At this time the late runs on Saturday nights were carried out by Clyde Marine Motoring's small vessels *The Second Snark* or *Kenilworth* under charter.

The *Loch Dunvegan* was not the only stranger to appear on the Rothesay-Wemyss Bay route. The Western Isles ferry *Claymore* (1978) had served on Cowal Games Saturday 1993 and had returned for a week in November 1994 to hoist-load while the Rothesay linkspan was out of action. The *Juno* was off service for a month in early 1996 and not only the *Claymore* but also the *Iona* (1970) substituted. The Islay ferry *Hebridean Isles* (1985) was to appear in August 2002 and the *Lord of the Isles* (1989) in May 2004 for special events. The ferry users were delighted to have such high-class ships on the station.

Skye ferry *Iona* arriving bow-in at Wemyss Bay while on an emergency relief sailing from Rothesay on 20 March 1996

John Newth

The former Skye ferry *Loch Dunvegan* alongside Rothesay Pier while on an emergency passenger only service to Wemyss Bay in April 1998

John Newth

The streakers were becoming quite elderly and as a result the passage time between Rothesay and Wemyss Bay was realistically increased to 35 minutes from the 1998/99 winter. Next season the Rothesay-Brodick excursion was, not surprisingly, discontinued but the streakers' cruises were extended to make up. The *Pioneer* simply remained throughout the day as secondary Rothesay ferry. 2000, however, saw the last of CalMac Clyde cruising. The result was that from 2001 the No 1A Roster in summer was restricted to three Dunoon runs daily and reliefs as required, with two streakers at Rothesay fulltime and one at Dunoon. In a sense this development was fortuitous as the *Juno* was out of service for seven weeks and the height of the summer and the *Pioneer* was available to deputise for her. When the *Juno* reappeared she was sporting her Gaelic name and the CalMac website on the white of her hull. This was over and above the Caledonian MacBrayne logo which the ships of the fleet had been carrying since 1984/85.

More New Tonnage – The Third Car Ferry Generation

An important development took place in 2002. From the start of the winter timetable that year a small catamaran, the *Ali Cat*, appeared from the Solent on charter to take the two morning and one evening Dunoon runs associated with the No 1A Roster - on a passenger only basis. This freed the streaker to spend her entire day at Rothesay and serve Bute at peak as well as off-peak periods. The charter was later extended. The little craft, after berthing trials, subsequently appeared at Rothesay itself, giving supplementary passenger runs during two peak weekends.
Meanwhile a new ship arrived in the CalMac fleet, the first of the third generation of car ferries, the *Coruisk*. Trailed as a sheltered water vessel, she was designed for the Mallaig-Armadale run in summer and Rothesay and Dunoon reliefs in winter. The consequence of the arrival of both the *Coruisk* and the *Ali Cat* was that the *Pioneer* was no longer required as a backup and she was withdrawn, her last rostered sailing from Rothesay being on 31 August 2003.

The entry into service of a sophisticated ship like the *Coruisk* was dogged by teething troubles, but by the time she found herself on the Rothesay route, following extensive trials, on 16 February 2004, she had settled down fairly well. Her passenger accommodation was athwartships

The chartered catamaran *Ali Cat* lying across the linkspan at Wemyss Bay while on passenger relief duties on the Rothesay route

John Newth

Oban ferry *Lord of the Isles* lying at Rothesay on 30 April 2004 while coping with the heavy traffic during the Isle of Bute Jazz Festival weekend

John Newth

above the open car deck. Thanks to regulations regarding the minimum height of the car deck above the water level and the clearance required for the larger lorries likely to require carriage, it was of greater height than normal. The result was that special gangways had to be commissioned for Wemyss Bay and Rothesay so that passengers would not be faced with too steep a climb when boarding.

By 2002, the *Saturn* and the other streakers, although they gave the impression that they could last forever, were in urgent need of replacement. Late in 2003 the Scottish Executive, who had since devolution replaced the Secretary of State as CalMac's sole shareholder, put funding in place for a new ship specifically for the Rothesay-Wemyss Bay crossing. According to EU rules the successful bidder had to be decided on a best value basis and as a result the £8.75m contract went to Poland, specifically to the Rementowa Group in Gdansk. Fitted with azimuthing thrusters and looking more like a conventional ship than the *Coruisk*, the new ship was to have a certificate for 450 passengers and was to be able to carry 60 cars. The facilities on board had been the subject of consultation with the ferry users of Bute. Any capacity problems experienced at Rothesay since the withdrawal of the *Pioneer* were set to evaporate. The new ship was launched – sideways - on 9 Feburary 2005 and was to be named *Bute*, seventh of the name on the Clyde and the name of one of the original Wemyss Bay paddle steamers of 1865. The naming ceremony was due to take place in Rothesay in early July. The *Saturn* was to be cascaded to Arran as a secondary vessel and the order for a sister ship to the *Bute* was eagerly awaited.

The arrival of the *Bute* in 2005 heralded the sixth generation of vessels to serve on the Rothesay-Wemyss Bay section in 140 years. The basic, austere paddlers of the Wemyss Bay fleet gave way to the early Caledonian steamers of the 1890s. They were largely replaced in the 1930s by new, modern vessels, with their paddles disguised so that they could be mistaken for turbine steamers, then considered superior. In response to the changing demands of the public, ships of the fourth generation, the ABC hoist-loading car ferries, were introduced in the fifties, but the conversion to roll-on roll-off operation in the seventies hastened their demise and ushered in thirty years of the streakers. The *Bute* (together with her relief ferry *Coruisk*) prefaced yet another

The first of the third generation car ferries, MV *Coruisk*, undergoing berthing trials at Wemyss Bay before entering service in February 2004

The launch of the new Rothesay ferry *Bute*, seventh of the name, from the Rementowa Shipyard, Gdansk, Poland, on 9 February 2005

Caledonian MacBrayne

improvement in the first decade of the new millennium, thanks to her greater capacity, her superior furnishings and her faster speed, as befits Caledonian MacBrayne's busiest route.

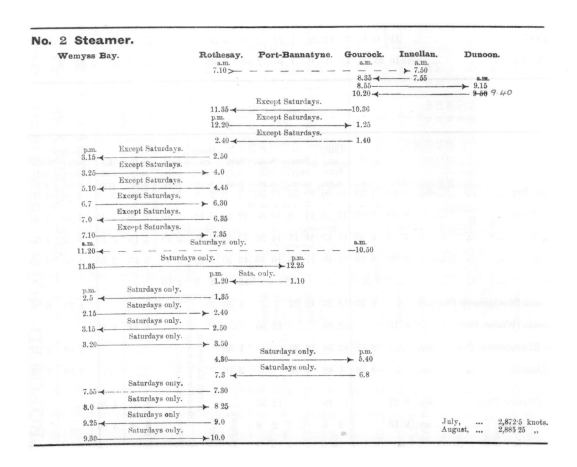

An example of a CSP steamer roster from 1912

ROTHESAY-WEMYSS BAY
SHIPS REGULARLY ON THE BASIC SERVICE IN SUMMER

P.S. Adela (1877)	1877 – 1889
P.S. Argyle (1866)	1866 – 1889
M.V. Arran (1954)	(1955 – 1957), 1958 – 1969
P.S. Bonnie Doon (1876)	1882 – 1885
P.S. Bute (1865)	1865
M.V. Bute (1954)	1955 – 1969, 1972 – 1974
M.V. Bute (2005)	2005 –
P.S. Caledonia (1889)	1915
P.S. Caledonia (1934)	1946 – 1949, 1952 – 1953
M.V. Cowal (1954)	1958 – 1969, 1972 – 1976
T.S. Duchess of Argyll (1906)	1950 – 1951
P.S. Duchess of Fife (1903)	1903 – 1914, 1920 – 1936
P.S. Duchess of Montrose (1902)	1903 – 1914
T.S. Duchess of Montrose (1930)	1940 – 1945
P.S. Duchess of Rothesay (1895)	1909 – 1915, 1920 – 1925, 1934 – 1935
P.S. Galatea (1889)	1890
M.V. Glen Sannox (1957)	1970 – 1971, 1975 – 1977, (1978-1988)
P.S. Iona (1864)	1917 – 1919
P.S. Ivanhoe (1880)	1916 – 1919
P.S. Juno (1937)	1937 – 1939
M.V. Juno (1974)	1986 –
P.S. Jupiter (1937)	1937 – 1939, 1946 – 1957
M.V. Jupiter (1974)	1986 –
P.S. Kyles (1865)	1865
P.S. Lady Gertrude (1872)	1872 – 1876
P.S. Lancelot (1868)	(1875 – 1889)
P.S. Largs (1864)	1865 – 1877

M.V. Maid of Skelmorlie (1953) [and others]	1958 – 1971
P.S. Marchioness of Br ane (1890)	1890 – 1907, (1908 – 1917)
P.S. Marchioness of Bute (1890)	1890 – 1907
P.S. Marchioness of Lorne (1891)	(1891 – 1914)
P.S. Mercury (1892)	1926 – 1933
M.V. Pioneer (1974)	(1989 –1993), 1994–2000, (2001-2003)
P.S. Queen-Empress (1912)	1936
M.V. Saturn (1978)	1978 –
P.S. Sheila (1877)	1877 – 1881
P.S. Venus (1852)	1869 – 1874
P.S. Victoria (1886)	1886 – 1889
P.S. Victory (1863)	1865 – 1870

Dates on right of table indicate Years of Service, brackets signifying a more minor role

ACKNOWLEDGEMENTS

In writing this outline of the service between Rothesay and Wemyss Bay from 1865 until the present day I have used my own research material but have also consulted the available literature, notably Iain C MacArthur's splendid history "The Caledonian Steam Packet Company", published by the Clyde River Steamer Club in 1971. Ian Maclagan's "Rothesay Harbour" (1976) was an additional valuable resource. The images are largely from my own collection, although of course few were actually taken by me. Each is attributed wherever possible. I am grateful to all who gave permission for their work to be published, to the staff of Caledonian MacBrayne for invaluable technical assistance and to those individuals and bodies who allowed items from their collections to be used. I also thank John Newth most sincerely for painstakingly reading the script and making several helpful suggestions.

Ian McCrorie
June 2005

The *Saturn* leaving Rothesay Bay and heading for Toward Lighthouse and Wemyss Bay

Gavin Young